For Sullivan

RODDY DOG
STARTS AT
SCHOOL

I said:

I've put my trousers on front to back and my jumper **outside in!**

Quickly, we got up and dressed,
but everything was in a muddle,

Dad tried to go out through
a window

BASH!

and Mum gave a cupboard a
goodbye cuddle.

As it was a busy morning, my dad said:

"we're running really late!"

So nobody noticed
that we left the dog
sitting at the
school yard gate...

He scampered into the classroom

and everyone said:

hello!

He read a book with my friends
and then in Music played cello.

So we all say:

Oh, Roddy Doggy Doo-Dah,

now we know who you are.

We're playing in the playground,

and we're learning lots today.

He struggled with Maths and English,

but really enjoyed PE.

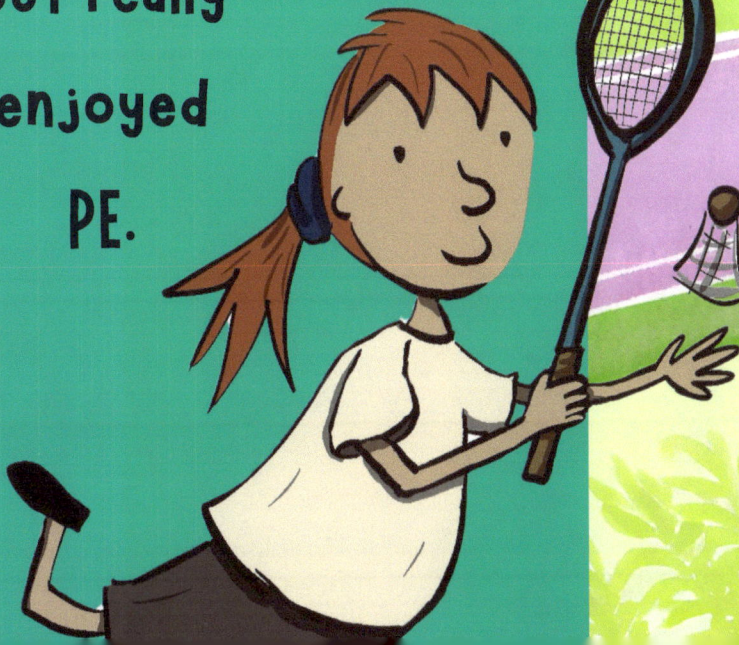

Art class got super messy,

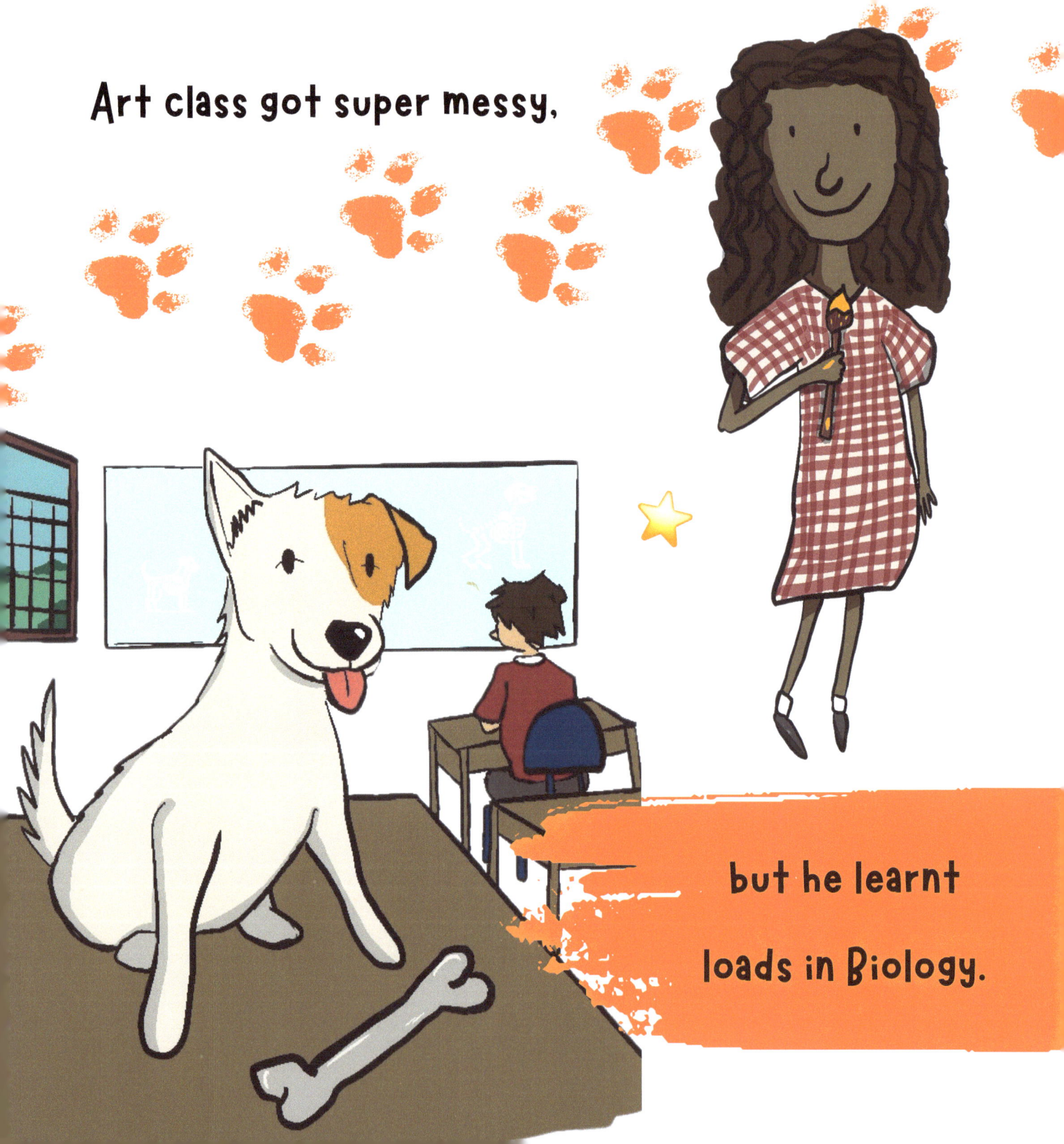

but he learnt
loads in Biology.

At lunch he
found a sandwich

and then helped to tidy
up the hall,

The teacher said:

What a good dog!

and put his picture on the wall.

So we all say:

Oh, Roddy Doggy Doo-Dah,

now we know who you are.

We're playing in the playground,

and we're learning lots today.

He ate everybody's homework,

and chased a bird into the gym.

And when it was time to get picked up,

he was looking so well-read.

But as soon as we got home, he yawned

and yawned
AND YAWNED

z z z Z

...and put himself straight to bed!

And we said:

Oh, Roddy Doggy Doo-Dah,

you didn't wander too far.

You're home at last with us now,

so rest your sleepy head.

THE END

WOOF!!

Things to do!

Find the correct resources for each subject...

GEOGRAPHY   **MATHS**   **ENGLISH**

SCIENCE   **PE**

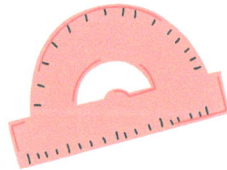

Reading Skills

Read the first line together and the second line independently.

The dog likes the ball.

| The dog | likes | the ball. |

I am reading a story.

| I am | reading | a story. |

The story is about a dog.

| The story | is about | a dog. |

There are 8 stars to find in the story

ABOUT THE AUTHOR

Charley is a writer, illustrator, and supporter of all things creative and imaginative. She lives with her family in sunny Sussex by the sea. Inspired by her years in teaching, Charley delights in wordplay and the creativity of language. Her catchy, engaging, and educational stories can be enjoyed by children and adults alike.

ABOUT THE DOG

Roddy Dog (Rodney Roberts) is a Jack Russell Terrier who loves adventurous walkies, playing with his ball, and sleeping in the warm and sunny spots. He is a very good boy.

AT'S RIGHT!

Charley Lockie

RODDY DOG SETS TO SEA

Charley Lockie

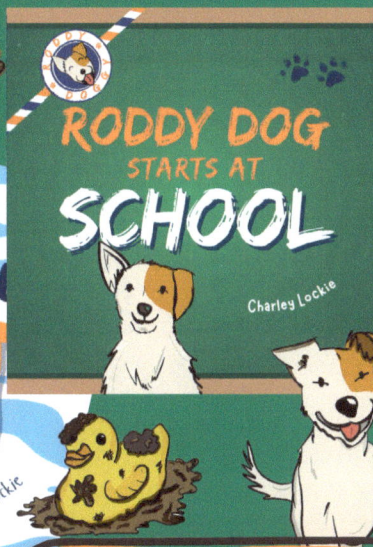

RODDY DOG STARTS AT SCHOOL

Charley Lockie

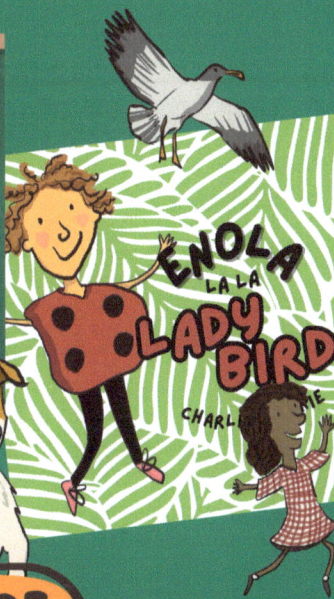

ENOLA LA LA LADY BIRD

CHARLEY LOCKIE

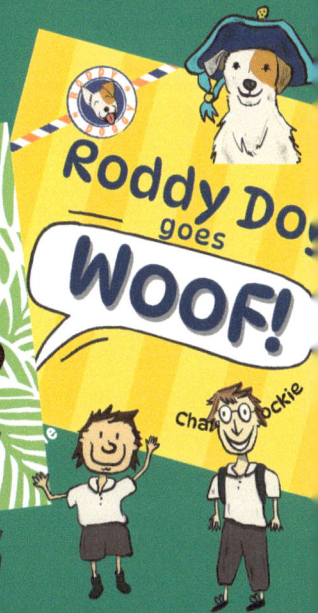

Roddy Dog goes WOOF!

Charley Lockie

READ MORE

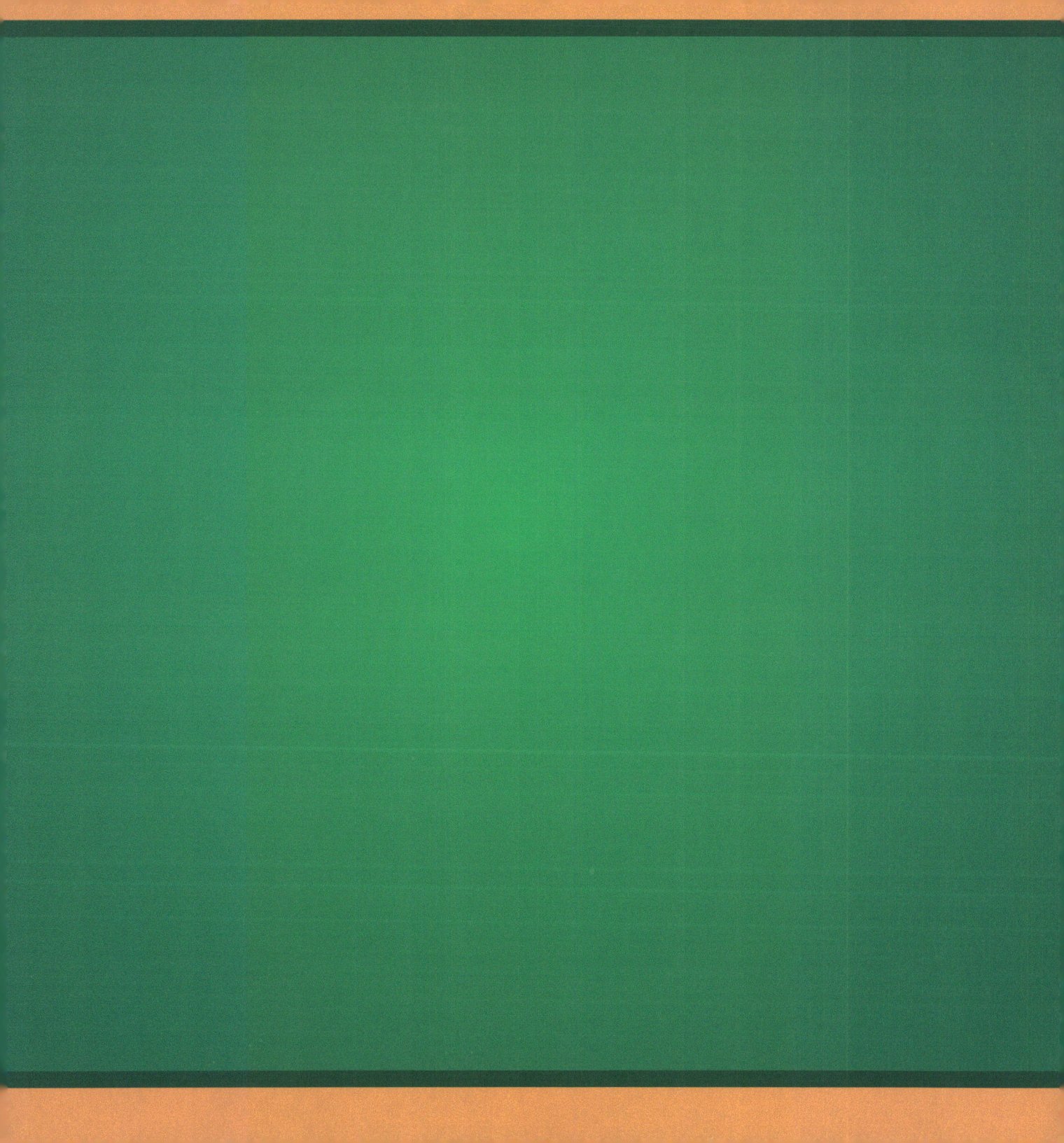

www.ingramcontent.com/pod-product-compliance
Lightning Source LLC
Chambersburg PA
CBHW041556040426

42447CB00002B/188